AF378791
AMX

KUWAIT
LUCAS

WHAT
CAR
IS THAT?
Peter Roberts
octopus

First published 1980 by
Octopus Books Limited
59 Grosvenor Street, London W1

ISBN 0 7064 1177 3

Produced by Mandarin Publishers Limited
22a Westlands Road, Quarry Bay, Hong Kong

Printed in Hong Kong

CONTENTS

INTRODUCTION

We are not far away from the year 2000. Many current driving licences are valid for several years into the next century. What cars shall we see on the roads during these threshold years? Will there be sudden changes in our method of travel? Will private cars be phased out now that fuel supplies are diminishing or have our engineering experts found the answer in another type of fuel? Will our cars be smaller, slower and quieter as the fashions and needs of the motorist change?

The story of the automobile is closely linked to the history of the past hundred years.

For many years the horse had been an instrument in the transport of war, the charger being the most formidable weapon. Journeys had been made at the pace of a horse's plodding walk, vital messages had been carried by a rider in the saddle. Suddenly, towards the end of the 19th Century, it all changed.

Why did the motor car appear when it did? The simple answer is that the engineers discovered how to bore an accurate hole in a piece of metal. Lathes had become more sophisticated. Near-perfect cylinders and pistons, bearings and shafts could now be made. Link this with the discovery that the hydrocarbon liquids produced by refining oil could be used as a fuel—and someone, inevitably, was going to invent the automobile . . .

The use of the car spread with astonishing speed. Over 2000 makes of car were registered in the USA by 1900. New improvements and additions poured into the patent offices. By about 1906 the motor car had settled into a standard pattern—front engine and

rear drive, like most of today's cars—and the engine operated much as it does today.

World War I speeded up technical advances to an even greater extent. Lightweight motors for airplanes were needed and designers began to use light alloys such as aluminium for parts of the engine. At the same time engine design became more compact and efficient, enabling smaller units to produce as much horsepower as older and much larger engines.

For the past half-century a lot of work has been done to improve established systems—better brakes, better carburation, suspension and so on, and innovations such as disc brakes, liquid or gas suspension etc, have done much to increase efficiency and safety. But in reality, despite all the improvements, we're left with the same old car. The family transport of a generation—even two generations ago —is not greatly different from that of today.

So what car are we to see in the near future? Today's internal combustion vehicles are amazingly well-designed and, particularly during the last few years, functional to use and beautiful to see. Even the ordinary family car—glance at a Renault 5, or an American Motors Pacer, or a Fiesta—has a clean shape and a sense of purpose in its concept. These are fine designs and clever engineering, but under the bonnet of every car lies a problem, the petrol-burning engine.

What car for the future? Electric? Steam? Fuel-cells? Chances are that until the end of this century we'll still have the old dirty, inefficient, petrol engine under the bonnet. Steam is clean but has starting problems, electricity is cheap but has speed-and-distance limitations; fuel-cells may be the answer but are not yet developed sufficiently.

Whatever the future brings, it will certainly present us with smaller cars, vehicles that are cleaner in terms of pollution, more economical in terms of fuel, and safer in terms of speed and control . . . but for the moment let's enjoy a glimpse of the cars of yesterday, elegant and tall, and some of today's products with their electronics and their sleek appearance and their fine engineering . . .

PIONEERS

Some of the first pioneers of mechanical road transport lived much earlier than the motor car itself. Leonardo da Vinci drew up plans for a self-propelled cart using passenger-muscle as its power nearly 500 years ago. An Italian engineer built a wind-driven road vehicle. A fifteenth century priest made a model steam vehicle that really worked, and many others took part in the groping and sometimes dangerous progress towards the transport of today.

Men of various walks of life contributed. Men like Volta, who managed to ignite a gas-and-air mixture, like engineer Cugnot who built and ran the world's first motor vehicle—and had the world's first motor accident when his enormous steamer ran into a wall in 1770; the Englishman William Murdock built steam models that led to full size trials, Richard Trevithick pioneered the steam carriage and de Rivaz who was granted patents in the early nineteenth century for a combustion engine for propelling road vehicles; all these have secure places in the pages of automotive history.

Then there were the later pioneers—German engineer Otto, whose study of gas engines led him to insert a fourth stroke in the engine sequence, one

FORD 'ACTION'

Every day new experimental machines are tested and developed in the world's motor manufacturers' closely-guarded research-and-development laboratories. Sometimes we see one on display at motor shows—an electric city car, a modern steam development, a new rotary-engined car, a hover-type vehicle. This one, seen at the Turin Show in 1978, is from Ford and it certainly looks as though it belongs to tomorrow's world.

that compressed the gas fuel before ignition it in the piston; Frenchman Lenoir, who pioneered the use of a gas engine in a crude vehicle he made in about 1863.

Thus the development of the first practical automobile was teetering on the brink of discovery . .

Two German engineers, working completely independently, at exactly the same time, in towns not 60 miles away from each other, came to almost identical conclusions. In 1886 Gottlieb Daimler tested his first petrol-fuelled internal-combustion-engine-driven horseless carriage, while just down the road at Mannheim Karl Benz was doing precisely the same thing with his three-wheeled *Patent Motor Wagen*. The first true automobile was born in those spring months, fathered by two pioneers who brought the motor car from its experimental stage to the reality of general use.

From the early experimental vehicles of Benz and Daimler stemmed the first motor car to be sold to the public. Benz concentrated on producing road vehicles and built improved versions of his three wheeler. He made his first four-wheeled car, the *Viktoria* (the name relating to victory over construction problems, not after the British queen) while Daimler, although making road transport, was building engines for boats, tramways—even airships—well before the 20th century.

Pioneering has never ceased. The story of the car is naturally punctuated by a long list of 'firsts'; pneumatic tyres, speed records, automatic lubrication, better carburation, automatic gear changing, more efficient running and more efficient stopping—a thousand improvements that are constantly being added to the design of the automobile as it becomes increasingly sophisticated.

BENZ PATENT MOTORWAGON

Above: This spindly three-wheeler, generally considered to be the first practical car, was built between 1885-6 by the engineer Karl Benz, one of the 'fathers of the motor car' at Mannheim in Germany. Patented on January 28th 1886, it had a four-stroke, one cylinder engine which developed just under one horsepower. Steered by tiller, and water-cooled, the water running through the cycle-type chassis, it could reach a speed of fourteen kilometres (nine miles) per hour, the pace of a trotting horse and carriage.

The engine had a large horizontal flywheel which governed the engine and ran at approximately 400 rpm. Benz had chosen the horizontal flywheel because he thought the gyroscopic effect of an upright flywheel would prevent the car from being steered properly. Benz's wife and two sons made the first long-distance run in the car to Pforzheim and back when they borrowed it while Benz was asleep one Sunday morning.

Benz developed his first car during the next two years, and by 1888 had brought out the first brochure and was selling them to the public as his patent motor car. 'A pleasant carriage which would run on either paraffin, petrol or naptha and which would climb a hill of the gradient of more than 1:16 when laden.' A local newspaper, the *Münchner Tagesblatt*, reported on the car thus, 'Without any sign of motive powers such as that generated by steam and without the aid of any human element such as is necessary with a velocipede, the vehicle rolled onwards, taking bends in its stride and avoiding all oncoming traffic and pedestrians. It was followed by a crowd of running and breathless youngsters.'

DAIMLER MOTOR CARRIAGE

Opposite above: Gottlieb Daimler, who lived at Bad Cann-statt, only a few miles from Karl Benz, produced a crude motorcycle in 1885, and his first automobile by 1886. His engine was a 1.1 hp unit which he installed in a light carriage, ordered from the coach-makers as a present for his wife's birthday so that he could fit his new engine into it in secrecy. Unlike Benz, who built and designed his engine and road vehicle as a single project, Daimler's dream was to produce engines that could drive various forms of transport. He went on to build a motor boat, tram car, and even fitted one of his units into an airship.

The previous year, 1885, Godfrey Daimler had made his first power driven vehicle—a boneshaker-type motorcycle with his single cylinder engine fitted inbetween the two crude wheels and a horse-type saddle draping the works. This 'single track' machine was patented on 29 August, 1885. It was the first practical motor vehicle to be so registered, and was certainly the world's first motorcycle. The horsepower of the engine was 0.5.

FORD QUADRICYCLE

Right: Henry Ford's work as an automobile builder dates from the winter of 1893 when he made his first primitive engine on his wooden kitchen table in Detroit. Three years later he built his first vehicle, a box-like frame on four bicycle wheels. It had no little luxuries such as brakes or a reverse gear, but the tiny two-cylinder engine could propel the crude quadricycle along at a breezy 40 km/h (25 mph). Henry sold it to a friend for $200 (£100).

LANCHESTER

Above: Built by Frederick Lanchester in Birmingham, England, the Lanchester has a firm pioneering claim in that its builder created it, like Benz, without reference to established carriage-building tradition, but planned it from the ground up as a motor car.

The first production model appeared in 1900. It had a horizontally-opposed air-cooled two-cylinder engine of ten hp, mounted centrally—all of which was very advanced for the motoring world of the day.

It was in effect the first British built, British designed motor car, and the Lanchester brothers, Frederick and George were eminent engineers of their day. Frederick has been working for the Forward Gas Engine Company in Birmingham and had studied internal combustion engineering in the United States. His younger brother George who had been apprenticed in the company was its works manager by the age of 18.

Pictured here is the 1903 Lanchester.

GARDNER-SERPOLLET STEAMER

Right: Steam cars were popular at the end of the last century, and vied with petrol as a means of propulsion. Frenchman Leon Serpollet was one of the great pioneer manufacturers of steam vehicles—one captured the world speed record in 1902 at 120.1 km/h (75.06 mph), a fantastic achievement at a time when anything over pony-trotting pace was wildly exciting. When Serpollet met a rich American, Frank Gardner he pursuaded him to finance a new factory, after which the cars were often called Gardner-Serpollet, like this model of about 1900. The flat-fronted appearance gave way to a fashionable bonnet in 1903—but all it contained was water for the boiler. The locomotive is producing the steam jet incidentally, not the car!

The Serpollet steam car played a part in the increasing popularity of motoring in Great Britain. The Prince of Wales had his first ride in a mechanical road vehicle when he went for a spin in a Serpollet in Bad Homburg in 1893. This experience fired his enthusiasm for motoring, and after his second ride (a trip in a Daimler motor car in 1896) the Royal heir was well and truly hooked.

CURVED-DASH OLDSMOBILE

Above: American Ransom Eli Olds first made electric cars, then turned to internal combustion (petrol) vehicles. The Olds works at Detroit, Michigan, burnt down in 1901, leaving just one experimental car untouched—the Oldsmobile Curved Dash Runabout. The company then concentrated on producing this single model—and made its fortune. The 'Merry Olds' was light and simple to drive, with its tiller steering and its tiny one-cylinder engine puffing along at 'one chug per telegraph pole'. It was the world's first mass-production vehicle long before Henry Ford developed the system.

MERCEDES TOURER

Above right: The first Mercedes cars were seen in 1901 when they won a series of motor sporting events in Nice in the South of France. Made by the German firm of Daimler, they were sold in France and named Mercedes after the eleven-year-old daughter of motor enthusiast, diplomat, and Daimler agent Emile Jellinek. By 1904, the date of the car shown here, they had proved time after time that they were technically far in advance of every other car of the day. They were copied by many other early motor manufacturers. This is the 32 hp 1904 Mercedes *Tourenwagen*.

ROLLS ROYCE SILVER GHOST

Right: The original Rolls-Royce Silver Ghost was one of the first 40/50 hp series designed and built by motor engineer Henry Royce in 1906, some two years after he had driven his first car out of his Manchester workshop. In 1904 Royce had met the Hon. Charles Rolls, who joined him in his motor manufacturing venture, and began work on the first Rolls-Royce cars. The 1906 40/50 hp was given a special aluminium-painted body for its Motor Show debut and named by Claude Johnson, the first managing director of the new company, the Silver Ghost.

Ghost was an apt name—as the leading British motoring journal *The Autocar* said: 'There is no realisation of driving propulsion; the feeling as the passenger sits either at the front or the back of the vehicle is one of being wafted through the landscape . . .' In May 1907 this car made a demonstration run from London to Scotland entirely in top gear, followed shortly by a marathon non-stop endurance run of 22,991 kilometres (14,371 miles), more than doubling the existing record for a non-stop run. When the car was subsequently examined, the cost of replacing worn parts came to £2. 2s. 7d. The superb engineering soon captured the interest of the world's wealthy who eagerly sought to purchase what became known as 'The World's Best Car'.

The original Ghost belonged for many years to a private owner, and when he died the car was given back to the company. It has today completed well over 400,000 miles and is still in excellent running order.

THE SILVER GHOST
AA
RR
ROLLS
ROYCE
GHOST CLUB
AX 201

FORD MODEL A

Above: There was no doubt about it, by 1926 the famous Model T Ford was on its way out, with sales slipping alarmingly during the year. Over 15,000,000 had been sold, and the old buggy was now far behind the latest advances in technology. It was finally brought to the end in May 1927.

The four-cylinder 3.3 litre Model A appeared some months later, a completely newly-designed modern vehicle. It looked so like its rich relative the Lincoln that many called the new car the 'Baby Lincoln'. Its wide colour range, after so many years of the old black Model T, gave sales an added boost at its launching. It was also offered in five different body styles. Made in the United States, Britain and Germany, over 5,000,000 little Model A's were sold before 1932 when Henry Ford began production of the bigger V8.

AUSTIN SEVEN

Above left: Herbert Austin's often ridiculed, but always popular tiny 747 cc Seven of 1922 was launched into a market that had long waited for 'real' motoring (as opposed to cycle-car motoring which had been fraught with hazards due to poor design and construction) at a reasonable cost. Here was the answer. The Austin Seven was Herbert's pet—he designed it himself, and he cherished it as if it were his own kin. He listened to advice and complaints, modifying and improving where necessary over the years. The early model weighed just over 450 kilogrammes (8.85 cwt), was just 266 cm (10.4 ft) long and had room for four small people. The car illustrated is a later Austin Seven.

MORRIS OXFORD

Left: William Richard Morris opened a bicycle repair shop in 1890 and by 1911 had designed his own car. In 1913 the first ten hp Morris Oxford, was delivered to a customer. Often called the 'Bullnose' it began a new trend of motor production in Britain for all the car's component parts were supplied to the Morris works by outside specialists, and assembled in Morris' factory. This picture clearly shows the 'Bullnose' front of the early Morris, so called after the rounded bullet shape of the radiator not, as many buyers imagined, after the animal.

The Cowley and the Oxford were soon selling in large numbers and Morris service stations sprang up all over Britain.

OPEL LAUBFROSCH

Above: Opel of Russelsheim had made sewing machines before turning to cars in 1899 when they built their Opel-Lutzmann Patent Motor Wagen. In 1924 Opel, by then the major automobile company of Germany, made their first quantity-produced car, this small two-seater 'Laubfrosch' (Tree-Frog) so-called as the first series was painted in a rather froggy green. The 951 cc four-cylinder 4/12 hp car was so like the Citroën 5CV of the time that the French company took Opel to Court over the design patents. The Laubfrosch became wildly popular in a Germany that whilst still recovering from the Great War, was just beginning to enjoy a mini-boom, with its public searching for a car that was modest, rugged, simple and reliable. The Tree-Frog filled these requirements perfectly.

THE WONDER WHEEL

Above right: Unlike many of the small vehicles produced during the twenties this curious conveyance, seen in a Dutch museum, was not popular with the growing motoring public. More of a humorous stunt car, or at best an experimental vehicle designed to prove the gyroscopic properties of a revolving wheel, the Wonderwheel, built in 1927, nevertheless has its place in automotive history.

Driven by a small two-stroke engine and controlled by a driver sitting within the circumference of the large wheel itself, the astonishing contraption really worked—although it could not be recommended for family outings. The multi-coloured smoke is for pictorial effect only.

This vehicle is part of a collection of historic cars now housed in the Lips Autotron, a large museum built on the lines of a Brabant farmhouse, near Drunen in Holland. Lips is one of the finest such collections in Europe.

CITROËN TYPE A & B

Right: Frenchman André Citroën had made gears and munitions during the World War I and by 1919 had re-designed his Paris factory to make small cheap cars, the first in Europe to be delivered to the customer complete with hood, spare wheel and accessories. Until then cars had been sold in chassis form, having coachwork designed later to the wishes of the buyer. The Citroen Type A, the first model to leave the factory, was a modest four cylinder 1.3 litre tourer, and was also the first car in Europe to be genuinely mass-produced. The fact that it had a top speed of just 64 km/h (40 mph) made little difference to its enormous popularity.

CITROËN
2416-E3
PARIS 150
Pierre Louys
JACOTIN
1, Faubᵍ de Marne
CHÂLONS-S/-MARNE

SPORTS CARS

Although nobody has ever managed accurately to describe a sports car, the term was much simpler to define in the days when almost all motor vehicles with a claim to high performance were open to the elements. When you saw one on the road, its driver's hair buffeted by the wind and his scarf trailing behind him like a banner, you knew that it was without doubt a sports car . . .

Today sportive vehicles come in a number of guises—and disguises. Who would have guessed when they first saw the Ford Cortina GT in the mid-1960's, that the modest, docile-seeming family

MERCEDES BENZ 'S'

During 1926 the Daimler and Benz motor companies amalgamated. The Daimler-Benz company, which makes the Mercedes-Benz range of vehicles was formed. In the same year the company brought out a high-performance tourer, the Mercedes Benz 'K'. The following year saw the S Model (often called the S26/120/180PS and in Britain the 36/220) with a large engine of $6\frac{1}{2}$ litres, a lower centre of gravity and a top speed of 166 km/h (103 mph). It was the top performance sports car of its time and was eagerly sought by wealthy enthusiasts for both road and track use.

car could leap from rest to 96 km/h (60 mph) in a brief twelve seconds ? And who would have imagined it would become one of the most successful winners of hard-fought races over the world's great circuits ? A glance at a BMW 320 saloon would not reveal its sporting character but look inside at its speedometer —and you will see that it is calibrated up to 224 km/h (140 mph) and its 0-96 km/h (0-60 mph) time is a rocketing 9.8 seconds.

Some sports cars of recent years look just what they are of course, a powerful engine on four wheels with a grudgingly-offered place for driver and passenger somewhere in the spaghetti of pipes and tubes. But most of the high performance cars made today have included in their design a great deal of luxury—the Aston Martin for instance, is beautifully upholstered, the Lancia coupé may be used for touring or fast trans-continental work, the Lotus range is as well appointed inside as most luxury cars.

So what is a sports car ? One of the best definitions is that it is a hybrid car, having some of the romance of the pure racing car yet practical enough to be used on the road as transport by the ordinary motorist . . . or one could say . . . a car in which performance is more important than carrying capacity . . . or perhaps . . . well you try!

HISPANO-SUIZA ALFONSO

Above: Swiss engineer Marc Birkigt designed this early sports car, the Hispano-Suiza (Spanish-Swiss) Alfonso, in honour of the Spanish king who was a keen motor fan.

The car's superb engineering and design established its claim to lasting fame. Powered by a 4-cylinder 3.6 litre unit which developed an exceptionally high (for its time) 64bhp it had a top speed of over 120 km/h (75 mph).

SALMSON 10 hp

Right: The Salmson was made in France by a company better known for its aero-engines. It was a rather flimsy vehicle, housing a 1100 cc motor and using simple chassis and suspension systems. Despite its apparent frailty in various forms it won many trophies during the 1920s.

ASTON MARTIN

Far right: This 1½-litre, long-chassis Aston Martin took fifth place overall at Le Mans in 1933, competing against many more powerful vehicles. Never in the big production league, Aston Martin considered they had a good year in 1933 when 105 cars were manufactured. Lionel Martin and Robert Barnford, its originators made their own car from parts of a Hispano-Suiza and a Coventry Simplex engine, and won the Aston Clinton Hill-climb in 1913.

JB 1982

LOTUS ECLAT

Below: Colin Chapman, founder of Lotus cars, has been in the business since 1948 when he re-bodied and tuned an ancient Austin Seven, entering it in several competitions. His cars and sporting successors are now legion, with championships in rallies, trials and motor racing events.

Today's Lotus cars made for use on the public highways are aimed at keen drivers with a liking for a sportive vehicle both in looks and performance. The 2-litre Eclat fills these requirements and offers more besides. Called a 2+2 (i.e. a two-seater with room in the back for two small passengers) the Eclat has air-conditioning and a maximum of 208 km/h (129 mph). Lotus cars have the knife-edged profile of the 1980s and the characteristics of a thoroughbred sports car, but bear the luxury fittings of more formal vehicles.

FIAT X1/9

Right: The Fiat X1/9 was first manufactured with a 1300 cc engine, and the modest 75 bhp unit took this small low-profile two-seater up to a surprising top speed of 169 km/h (105 mph). The mid-engine design (the engine is placed a little farther forward than it would be in a true rear-engined car) helps stability without the need for expensive chassis engineering and gives the car the qualities of handling usually reserved for vehicles twice the cost. When first seen in 1972 its flip-up lights, removable roof-panel (it fits into the boot) and front spoiler were exciting innovations.

LANCIA MONTE CARLO

Above left: Italian driver-designer Vincenzo Lancia built his famous Lancia Lambda with its monocoque body in 1921. The basic parts of the body itself formed the rigid frame of the car, instead of the two heavy 'railway line' girders on which cars were first built. The Lancia is a quality car with good handling and lively performance. This one, the Monte Carlo, first seen in 1974, is one of the mid-engined cars that look practical and sportive. The 2–litre engine gives it a noisy 192 km/h (120 mph) top speed. The Monte's transverse (sideways) engine is behind the two seats and like all so-called mid-engined cars is tucked as far forward as possible, although it could still be called a rear engine.

FORD CAPRI TURBO

Right: This specially-built 380 horsepower turbocharged Ford Capri first raced at Hockenheim in Germany in 1978. It looks something like the off-the-peg Capri, but make no mistake, this is an animal of a different breed. It is lower and much wider than the standard model, with its body made of a fibreglass that is about ten times as expensive and only just half the weight of the normal pressed steel bodywork.

The Capri Turbo's large front spoiler runs the full width of the car, and the frontal area of this aerodynamic vehicle is so small that the engine-cooling radiators have been put

inside the ventilated rear-wheel arches.

The low front area and the bonnet slope also help develop 'ground effect', the downward air pressure that keeps the car 'glued' to the road at high speeds.

ASTON MARTIN VB

Above right: A British thoroughbred of the road, the Aston Martin has always been a car for the sportsman. With more recent additions it has also become very much a luxury vehicle (this one has automatic gear change) without losing any of its sporting image.

A sports car with an automatic gear change would have been a strange thing a few years ago, but since some of the world's most gruelling races have been won by cars with automatics no-one now dares to say that they are just for motorists who are not interested in driving . . .

The Aston Martin V8 has a colossal punch on what might be called 'take-off', for it does almost that, taking just seven seconds to reach 97 km/h (60 mph) from being stationary. A joy to drive well, this car with its great power, demands thoughtful and disciplined control.

Always known for sportive vehicles, Aston Martin introduced their most famous racing model, the DBR, in 1956. This car developed into an extremely competitive machine, taking Carroll Shelby and Roy Salvadori to a win at Le Mans in the same year.

DATSUN

NFC 263T

DATSUN 280ZK

Above left: The latest of the sports line from Japan, this Datsun 280ZX is the current version of its honourable ancestor, the 260Z. This one is a 2 + 2 a two-seater with another seat at the rear for a couple of passengers who are not too worried about comfort. The 280ZX has a 2.8–litre engine, larger than its predecessor, and uses a fuel-injection system. Power steering and electric windows put it in the de-luxe class, and an award as 'Imported Car of the Year' in the United States of America in 1979 ensured its popularity.

If American demand for the 280ZX is similar to that for the 260Z this model will, like the earlier one, be very difficult to buy in Europe in the coming years.

MGB

Below left: They say that the MG is more a way of life than a motor car. Certainly it is a car that does not change very much, and the MGB is bought by many people who have previously owned one of the marque. The MGB has been with us now since 1963, ten years longer than its immediate forerunner the MGA, proving its undoubted popularity in both Europe and the USA. The MG sports car has been a favourite in Britain for more than half a century and despite the fact that sometimes its design has lagged behind others of similar breed, it is still Britain's most successful enthusiasts' car.

The MG was born in 1924. Cecil Kimber had been managing the increasing numbers of Morris garages that had sprung up in the twenties. By 1922 he had begun fabricating special bodies for Morris cars, particularly for the 1.8 litre Oxford.

JAGUAR E TYPE

Above right: During the 1950s the great Twenty-Four Hours Endurance Race held annually at Le Mans in France was won no less than five times by a single British make. For three successive years, 1955, 1956 and 1957, a spectator at the race would hear, as the long round-the-clock race came to its conclusion, the crowds lining the circuit chanting the name of the approaching winner ' . . . Jaguar . . . Jaguar . . . c'est JAGUAR!' and the C-type or D-type racing version of the car from Coventry would flash past the chequered flag in the afternoon light.

The E-type Jaguar, the direct descendent of those famous winners was launched in 1961 as a 3.8–litre 265 bhp sports model of sleek cat-like line and very high speed. The E-type pictured here is the 1971 V12 version.

The E-type has been out of production for several years now, and has become a much sought after car among enthusiasts of the thoroughbred class. Many consider it to have been the ultimate in road sports motoring. The last of the production models had lost their edge slightly, as emission controls took away the last few horsepower. Its distinctive shape and high speed put it in the top class.

LUXURY MOTORING

Today most luxury motor cars have installed in their 'living area' objects designed to make travelling-time pass more quickly. The passengers and the driver can be kept in a comfortable temperature, or they may be soothed by taped music.

Luxury motoring is in many ways taken for granted today. Many years ago, few cars had even that most basic of luxuries, an electric warm-air heater, and when it was introduced it was considered luxury indeed; foot-warmers designed rather like hot-water bottles were suddenly out-dated. Then radio appeared. Passers-by would crowd around a parked car that had its wireless receiver switched on; today almost every car we see has a silver wand that captures the sound waves. Now cassette players can be fitted into the car and we have stereo music to travel with—even quadraphonic if we wish. Colour television in the passenger compartment brings the ultimate in luxury to some of the specially-designed larger luxury cars.

When motor cars first appeared all were craftsman-built and all motoring was luxury motoring. Only very few people could afford to buy an automobile, and those that possessed one used it almost entirely for pleasure. Motoring was considered to be one of the many sports of the wealthy, something to be indulged in between the hunting season and the warmer tennis months.

Now if you take a peep into the next Mercedes or Bentley or large BMW that you see parked on the road, you may admire the carpeting, the upholstery, the multi-positioned front seating, the complex in-car entertainment equipment and you will realize that taste and craftsmanship can still be seen in a modern product.

BMW 3-SERIES

This BMW is one of the German manufacturer's 3-Series. The Munich company (Bayerische Motoren Werke) makes several models clothed in the same body, including the 316 (1½ litre) the 320 (2 litres) the 320i (2 litres with fuel injection) and the latest addition, the 323i (2.3 litres with fuel injection). Since 1977 the 320, the most popular model, has had a new six-cylinder engine giving the car a very lively acceleration and a fast-cruising speed of 160 km/h (100 mph). This high speed is often used over quite long periods of driving on motorways in European countries which do not operate a speed limit.

DUESENBERG

Above: Fred and August Duesenberg had come to America with their parents as children in the 1880s. By 1920 they had made the first car to bear their name, the Model A. Racing experience enabled them to build skilfully and the car was one of the first with a straight-eight cylinder engine. It was also the first car in the United States to be fitted with hydraulic brakes. The Duesenberg Model J, the best known of these great American cars, was bigger, faster and more expensive than other American cars. This beautiful sleek monster, favourite of the great film actors of the day, could travel at 187 km/h (116 mph) in top gear and gave 265 bhp—twice as much power as its nearest rival. The following model, the SJ (a 1937 model is seen here) was even more astonishing. This car, launched in 1932, developed a shattering 320 bhp and could move away from rest to 160 km/h (100 mph) in a roaring 17 seconds. Today, Duesenberg replicas are being built in America and are being bought as fast as the makers can produce them.

There were two attempts to revive the company—once in 1947 and again in 1966. Both attempts were unsuccessful.

ROLLS ROYCE

Lower left: If you ask anyone at Rolls-Royce if they have a museum to house some of their historic cars, you'll always get the same answer. There *is* no Rolls-Royce museum because all their cars are still in use. If this is not quite accurate, it's near enough the case—there are very few Rolls-Royce cars (never call them 'Rolls-Royces' if you want the approval of the makers, although you may call one a 'Roller' today) that cannot be driven on the road with a little coaxing, even the first ones of long-ago Edwardian days. The 1911 Silver Ghost limousine seen here has done a lifetime of travelling and is still driven regularly to rallies, and is confidently seen out and about several times during the year. Its nickname is 'Strikes' and it is used as a town carriage by its owner Mr Cecil Bendall. With only small changes, the Silver Ghost remained the company's only model until 1922, when the 'Baby Rolls', the Twenty, was introduced to the discerning public.

AUSTRO DAIMLER

Below: Gottlieb Daimler, one of the fathers of the motor car, set up a factory in Austria to make about a hundred cars a year. Later, the Austro-Daimler firm broke away from its parent and was headed by a man whose name is as well-known today as it was in 1906 when he took over as director—Dr Ferdinand Porsche.

Early A-D tourers made a fine reputation for the firm, even though some of them looked like gigantic upturned bathtubs.

Dr Porsche, who also designed the brilliant Volkswagen and the earlier Porsche models, then produced a small racing car for A-D. He followed that with some notable sporting vehicles; this is the ADR8 of 1932, a dignified and luxurious model, the marque's only eight-cylinder car. The Austro-Daimler company finally stopped making cars in 1936, and this is one of the few left. It can always be recognized by its round radiator and the figure eight above the badge on the bonnet.

1900 TU

S · AP 1358

BENTLEY T

Left above: Bentley made some of Britain's most distinguished sports cars in the Twenties but the company became bankrupt in 1931 and was taken over by Rolls-Royce. Since then the luxurious Rolls-Royce and Bentley models have been made side by side with differences only in details. The Bentley T, for instance, is practically identical to the Rolls-Royce Silver Shadow.

The model was introduced in 1965 with a V8 engine of 6230 cc, increased to 6750 cc in 1970. It is a big relaxing four-door, five seater, 519 cm (17 ft) long, and capable of a loping 190 km/h (118 mph) with automatic transmission, power steering and braking. It has air conditioning, electrically operated windows and electrically adjustable front seats, and is equipped with quadraphonic tape-playing equipment.

MERCEDES-BENZ 350 SL

Left below: Open-topped cars are a diminishing breed, and the 350 SL is particularly unusual today in being a luxury, two-door, two-seater convertible. Comfort-lovers can, however, buy an optional hard-top. The car was introduced by Mercedes, Germany's most prestigious manufacturer, in 1971.

Its V8 engine of 3499 cc will carry the 439 cm (14 ft 4 in) car along at 205 km/h (127 mph). The steering is power-assisted, but being a car for enthusiasts, it usually has a manual gearbox. Automatics can be fitted however, along with air-conditioning and electric windows.

A feature that has since become popular is the completely removable coupé roof, which has been an aesthetic success in this car.

At the end of 1971 the 350 SLC coupé followed the extremely successful SL.

DAIMLER DOUBLE-SIX

Above: Daimler cars have been used regularly by the British Royal Family since the early part of this century, and although the company was taken over in 1960 by Jaguar (which has a somewhat racier image) the Daimler Double-Six still retains its dignified appearance, with its leather upholstery and figured walnut fittings proper to a marque which began in 1893.

The Double-Six, launched in 1972, gets its name because it has a V12 engine instead of the six-cylinder units customary in other models. This car has a capacity of 5343 cc. It is a generous five-seater, with a dramatic 225 (140 mph) performance, with automatic transmission and power steering for VIP's in a hurry. Twin fuel tanks are built into the rear wings to cope with its thirst.

Electrically-operated windows make it simpler for the occupants to acknowledge cheers from crowds!

CITROËN CX 2400 PALLAS

Top: You could buy five of these for the price of the Bentley or Aston Martin on the previous pages, and two for less than the cost of the Mercedes, Daimler or Jaguar. The engine is a modest four-cylinder of 2347 cc.

Yet it is a pace-setter, with its strange aerodynamic styling and unique self-levelling hydro-pneumatic suspension system. Heavy loads make no difference to the Citroën Pallas for it automatically adjusts its suspension so that the body remains at a constant height.

Introduced in 1976, this model has a five-speed gearbox, powered steering, tinted windows and electrically-adjustable external mirrors. Top speed is 181 km/h (112 mph).

ASTON MARTIN LAGONDA

Above: The driver of this rakish four-seater limousine is surrounded by electronic instrumentation. There are light displays behind black plastic panels, and touch-sensitive switches (no pressing or turning needed) even for the automatic transmission selection. This sophisticated and expensive machine, launched in 1976, also has two-position clutch, brake and accelerator pedals. The 5340 cc V8 engine gives a silky 225 km/h (140 mph) performance.

JAGUAR XJS

Right: This was the most sought-after car in the world when it was first offered for sale in 1975 and waiting lists were long. The distinctive aerodynamic body is unmistakably Jaguar, and has a two-door, 2 + 2 coupe styling. The V12 5343 cc engine is fuel-injected to give a top speed of 241 km/h (150 mph). No fewer than 18 warning lights monitor all the main functions, and the car is air-conditioned with electrically-operated, tinted windows.

ONE WAY
ONE WAY
EUROPEAN

MINIS AND BEETLES

Small is beautiful, is today's maxim in the motor industry. The tinier the car the less fuel and space it requires, and the less it poisons our atmosphere, the more acceptable it is in an age crowded with pollution problems. Early in the story of the automobile, small cars brought mobility to the many who could not afford anything larger.

Cyclecars, narrow and spindly wire-and-bobbin affairs that could be highly dangerous, had been sold since Edwardian days, but the public had long sought a small car that looked like a car. Herbert Austin gave them, in 1922, the Austin Seven.

But the most famous, if not the first, small car that could be termed a 'real car' was the astonishing Mini which first captured the imagination of the world in 1959. Designer Issigonis had scribbled his original ideas on the back of an envelope, developing them into the little transverse-engined front-wheel drive, rubber-sprung square-edged Mini. It was so different, so useful, and so roomy for such a small car that

everybody wanted to own one.

There are now several types of Mini. The French Renault 5 is an example that is copied by other makers. The small General Motors Vauxhall Chevette, the VW Polo, and the Fiestas from Ford are all modern expressions of the maxim 'small is beautiful'.

Then there was the unforgettable Beetle. Designed originally by Dr Ferdinand Porsche in the 1930s, this car was born into the aftermath of war. The factory had been ruined and the workers dispersed, but somehow production restarted, and in a few short years the VW Beetle had outstripped any other model in production numbers.

All the signs are that minis and beetles will be with us for a long time . . .

RENAULT 5

The Renault 5 appeared in the early 1970s and was seen as a little car that would meet the changing demands of motoring as world fuel supplies dwindled.

The car is made with a number of different engine sizes; 845cc, 956cc (Renault 5TL), and 1289cc (Renault 5GTL). The higher performance Renault TS has the same 1289 cc engine as the GTL but has its power boosted by a more complex carburettor.

This French car is simple to drive, is quiet at high speed and its suspension gives a clean, smooth ride. Today, many owners of larger vehicles have changed to cars which could be called 'minis' (although most are bigger than the original British Mini) such as the Fiat 127, the Peugeot 104, the Datsun Cherry and Ford Fiesta.

VOLKSWAGON 'BEETLE'

Above: The waistcoated figure in the centre of the group in the foreground is the great car designer Dr Ferdinand Porsche. The scene is his home in Stuttgart, Germany in 1936. The cars, which he built in his own garage, were early attempts by Porsche and his workers to make a small, cheap family vehicle for Hitler's Germany. In the picture also are engineers and government officials who have come to examine the prototype machines. This car was to be called by several names including *Kleinauto* and the *Strength-through-joy* car before it became known as the Volkswagen (which means 'people's car').

Almost immediately after the war, the Volkswagen factory at Wolfsburg, near the East German border was completely devastated but was soon built up again.

FORD Y MODEL

Above left: The dream car for the family man of the 1930s who did not own a car, was this British-built Ford Y 8 hp Model. Often remembered as the £100 Ford, it was the first saloon car ever to be offered at such a low price. The 933cc Y Model also has another claim to fame—it was the last car in which the elderly Henry Ford himself had a personal hand in designing. It was a little like Henry too—rugged, simple, with inexpensive tastes.

The car was sold in Britain from 1932. It was the first true British Ford, and the first car to be made in Ford's Essex factory. By 1938 it had been developed into the more modern Anglia.

ROVER EIGHT

Left: Here is the once-famous Rover air-cooled flat-twin-cylinder Eight. Its engine's two cylinders lay on their side with the crankshaft between them. As the engine compartment was narrow, the ends of the cylinders stuck out each side, and were hidden under cowls so that nervous passengers could not see that they often glowed cherry red when working hard!

This small 988cc British car was very popular during its time of production—from 1920 to 1925. As this model was hardy and simple it was seen on the roads for many years after it had ceased being made.

CITROËN 2CV

Left above: The tough but stark Citroën 2CV (often called the *Deux Chevaux*—'two horses') was designed by Pierre Boulanger. His instructions were to build a car of very basic design to suit the needs of a farmer who has to take his eggs to market over rough French lanes and who cannot afford to break one of them. 'We want four wheels under an umbrella with springs,' they told him. The 2CV took 10 years to design. The first experimental cars were made in 1938 and tested in France. Then World War Two interrupted work on the car as Citroën turned over to military production.

Eventually the little 'corrugated iron' car made its first public appearance in the Paris Show of 1948, and was bought by farmers and townsfolk alike. Everyone was short of money in the post-war period and the economy of the tiny 375cc engine was a great encouragement to purchase the little grey Citroën.

It doesn't look very different today, although its engine is bigger and its paintwork more colourful. It still has nicknames like *Ugly Duckling* and *Ragamuffin*.

Its popularity is often hard to understand. It was never a status symbol; it was never class conscious, but it was bought by all sections of first French and then European society, despite its square ugly looks.

MINI

Left below: When the British Mini appeared in 1959 (then called either the Morris Mini-Minor or the Austin Seven) all other small cars were out-dated and out-classed. Designer Alec Issigonis had slipped the little 848cc engine sideways into the front of the car to drive the front wheels, giving a lot more room inside the car. Other innovations included gearbox and transmission as part of the engine assembly, and rubber suspension, independent to each wheel. The car proved so useful on the road and so successful in rallying and racing that it is still selling well 20 years later in several forms and engine sizes.

Its reasonable price, easy parking and low fuel-consumption still make it an ideal car for city drivers.

FIAT 850

Above: Another small car to arrive exactly when it was needed was the rear-engined Fiat 850, seen here in a 1964 advertising poster. The girl in the poster was painted by the famous artist Pietro Annigoni and the Fiat was craftsmen designed by a team of 300 artists and craftsmen. It was introduced in the mid '60s, just when motorists in Europe were beginning to realize that fuel-saving was to be a part of their lives, as the world's oil wells would not always gush out cheap oil for refining into petrol.

There were three models of the 850; the saloon, seen in the illustration, the coupe, a pretty little 2 + 2 vehicle, and the two-seater open sports car, which in true European tradition is called a *spider*.

WORKING HORSEPOWER

The wartime birth of the Jeep started a trend. Once peace had returned it was quickly noticed that old Jeeps were very useful indeed down on the farm. Italian farmers could be seen at the wheel of battered, bullet-holed ones in the late 1940s, drawing harrows, rakes, ploughs—anything that would have been towed over the field by a horse in former years. Also, whilst hauling a multitude of farm goods, the maid-of-all-work four-wheel-drive Jeep could cover country difficult even for a tank to negotiate.

Today there are many kinds of utility or multi-purpose vehicles with four-wheel drive and two gear-ratios, giving them in effect eight gears. The old plain-jane Jeep has grown much prettier too, with looks and a shine that would grace the drive of any home from a local semi-detached to the White House. Their prime purpose is still to traverse country that would be too hazardous for the normal car, but now these chunky cross-country vehicles are also coveted status symbols.

MERCEDES G RANGE

Early in 1979, Mercedes-Benz of Germany brought out a new four-wheel drive cross-country passenger vehicle. Like the Range Rover and the American Jeep-type vehicles, this new workhorse is more luxurious than strictly necessary for farm work, and like the Range Rover will probably be used as much in urban regions as over the fields. Mercedes now offer four different models, two driven by petrol engines and two by diesel, and several types of body cater for a host of different jobs. Built in Austria the Mercedes 230G and its companions can travel over some alarming country (see illustration) fully living up to the 'G' in its name—*Gelandefahrzeug*—which could be translated as the Go-everywhere-car.

JEEP CHEROKEE

Above: Apart from the fact it has four-wheel drive, there is not much resemblance between this handsome estate wagon of 1979 and the Jeep of World War II. The Jeep has come a long way since then and this vehicle would look as much at home outside a four-star hotel as on a farm, but the four-wheel drive gives it the versatility that an increasing number of people require.

It comes in two- or four-door form and will carry six people at up to 145 km/h (90 mph). The standard power unit is a six-cylinder 4288 cc engine with a three-speed gearbox, but the Cherokee can also be obtained with automatic transmission. The Cherokee tips the scales at a solid 2 tons, and the mileage per gallon is an expensive 13.5, under what could be called 'normal' conditions. Such is the Cherokee's power that it can leave several types of sports cars on the rear horizon on take off.

JEEP CHIEF

Right: Top of the Jeep range, the Chief, a super-Cherokee, is America's answer to Britain's Range Rover (see page 51)

which has sold all over the world. Although its four-wheel drive is a permanent feature, it can eat up a motorway at 160 km/h (nearly 100 mph) as well as travel cross-country with the agility of a fast-tracked vehicle. The engine is a V8 of 5899 cc.

The Chief has only two doors, but it can carry up to six passengers, having what is an unusual sight today, a bench-type front seat.

JEEP RENEGADE

Above: The Renegade Roadster is more recognisably a Jeep; it isn't very pretty and still has a military look about it, particularly at the front end. It also retains the traditional canvas top.

A squat 351 cm ($11\frac{1}{2}$ ft) in length, seating only two, its four-wheel drive makes it a lusty little workhorse. The standard six-cylinder 4228 cc engine gives it a top speed of 125 km/h (78 mph) but with an optional eight-cylinder 4982 cc engine it will reach 135 km/h (84 mph).

Options include an all-metal or half-metal top, heavy duty suspension for rough country use, and a racing-style roll bar that completes its 'tough' look.

MILITARY JEEP

Right: The quarter-ton utility vehicle of World War Two got the name Jeep from the letters GP which stand for General Purpose. It was born in 1940 when the American Willys-Overland company was given a contract to build 16,000 models. Larger orders followed and Willys was joined in producing them by the great Ford concern. By the end of the war, 639,000 Jeeps had been made and they had served in every theatre of operations.

With six forward and two reverse gears allied to its four-wheel drive, the Jeep could go almost anywhere. It was used as a reconnaissance car, a gun carrier, an ambulance and, heavily armed with machine guns, it penetrated behind enemy lines on special operations. It was carried to battle zones in gliders. There was also an amphibious version and another with flanged wheels which ran on railway lines. The wartime German army produced its own copy of it, the Kubelwagen.

LAND ROVER

Below: Millions of servicemen had seen and appreciated the virtues of the Jeep during the war, and it was inevitable that such a vehicle should be harnessed to peacetime use. The most successful version has been Britain's Land Rover, launched in 1948 and developed continuously ever since, though it still has a military look with the spare wheel mounted on the bonnet top.

It can be used in two- or four-wheel drive and with a choice of low or high gear ratios. On the road it is a rather spartan form of transport giving a hard ride, but away from roads it is a master of every kind of terrain. Farmers were among the first to put it to use, crossing ploughed fields and climbing heather-covered moorland in all weathers. The four-cylinder 2286 cc engine gives it a speed of 106 km/h (66 mph).

Although only 362 cm (about $11\frac{3}{4}$ ft) long, it can carry seven passengers or a load of 680 kg (1499 lb). There is also a bigger version with a six-cylinder 2625 cc engine which can carry twelve people. Diesel versions of the Land Rover are also made.

RANGE ROVER

Left: No safari expedition and no motorized band of explorers is complete today without a Range Rover. It is the ultimate in four-wheel drive vehicles, combining the ruggedness of the Land Rover with the comfort and speed of a Rover saloon.

When it was introduced in 1970, customers queued for delivery. It has snob appeal; it was fashionable to drive one, even if it was required to travel no further from a road than necessary for a forest picnic. Others have been used to cross deserts. It is massively strong vehicle, 447 cm (14½ ft) long, capable of moving five people or a load of 780 kg (1720 lb) at 154 km/h (96 mph). The V8 engine of 3528 cc is the same one that is used in big Rover saloons; an overdrive unit which was introduced in 1978 can give it sixteen forward and 4 reverse ratios.

Until recently the Rover company had almost cornered the off-road market and for years the public had had to wait for their deliveries for some time. Today, despite its many competitors, the cachet of the Range Rover remains.

THE FAST ONES

When Karl Benz began testing his first car in the suburbs of Mannheim, the police forbade him to trundle along any faster than six kilometres an hour (4 mph). This walking pace was certainly not fast enough for Benz, so he approached the Minister of the Interior for permission to increase his maximum speed, taking the dignitary for a demonstration ride in the three-wheeler. It is said that Herr Benz had a quiet word with the local milkman before the ride. The result was that when the inventor and minister were plodding along at the maximum speed limit, the milkman trotted his horse-and-float past them, laughingly calling 'What's up—can't you go any faster?' Annoyed, the minister said to Benz: 'Well, can't you?' 'Certainly, Minister', replied Benz, 'but your regulations won't allow it'. Said the Government official: 'Hang the regulations!' and the speed limit was raised there and then.

Human nature did not change much over the following years. As soon as one young sportsman acquired a car another would want to pit his skill and his vehicle against him. Motor racing was born.

WINGFOOT EXPRESS

The land speed records date from 1898 when 63.13 km/h (39.24 mph) was the fastest man had travelled on land. The 'jet age' arrived with Craig Breedlove flashing over Bonneville Flats in the USA in his three-wheeled jet Spirit of America, at 655.72 km/h (407.45 mph). This car was not driven through its road wheels, but was 'pushed' by its ex-military jet engine, which initially caused controversy. American Tom Green, seen in the jet-propelled Wingfoot Express, was the second of the 'jet-set' to establish a new land speed record, reaching 664.97 km/h (413.20 mph) in 1964.

The sport grew rapidly, speeds rose dizzyingly until, only just a few brief years into the 20th century, racing cars were exceeding 150 km/h (93 mph). Racing on closed circuits was started when horrific accidents began to make it impossible to race on open roads.

Regulations about maximum engine sizes were introduced to reduce the cars from the gigantic monsters they had become down to more reasonable proportions. Fuel consumption regulations further tightened the development of racing vehicles, channelling their technical progress into ways that could help the ordinary car's development.

Today Grand Prix, or Formula One regulations state that the single-seater cars we see competing for the world championship are restricted to an engine size of 3 litres, or $1\frac{1}{2}$ litres supercharged, and a minimum weight of 500 kg.

Running parallel with the development of motor sport has been the long see-sawing contest for the land speed record. The first record, in 1898, was set up at the then exhilarating speed of 63.13 km/h (39.24 mph) by an electric car. Just eight years later the record stood at 196 km/h (121.57 mph), over three times as fast. Until 1964 the land speed record was recognized only if set by a car whose power was transmitted to its road wheels. Then, with the introduction of jet-propelled cars, the regulations were forced to change, allowing American Gary Gabelich to take the record in 1970 at 1014.5 km/h (630.38 mph) in the rocket-powered Blue Flame, a land speed record that stood until 1979.

ERA

Top: During the early 1930s British racing cars did not feature in the lists of winners on international racing circuits. The Brooklands track, built in 1907 had encouraged cars to be made specially for the banked track, and few could compete internationally on an ordinary road circuit.

Humphrey Cook, a rich amateur racer, and Raymond Mays, a driver who had developed his own car and held a number of hill-climbing records, formed the English Racing Automobile company (ERA) and in 1933-34 built a 1½-litre supercharged racer, selling at £1,500, which could compete in the 'voiturette' (light car) class abroad.

The ERA became a great success in this field. By 1937, the peak year (the cars had been greatly improved, with the power output raised by a Zoller supercharger), ERA had scored 14 racing success to Mercedes' 7—and this from a tiny organisation.

Mays, who later founded the BRM racing car team, took the ERA to dramatic wins, mainly in hillclimbing. This is a contest in which cars start separately and race against the clock up a twisting hillside road. ERA cars may still be seen racing today in special events.

A RACING TRACK

Above right: Early motor racing took place on public roads. As the speed of the dare-devil racers increased, disasters became commonplace. Imagine a huge steel-and-wood monster of twelve litres (five times as large as an engine of today's average car) hurtling down a rutted road at 130 km/h (80 mph) with large crowds on either side. An accident due to these conditions occurred during the Paris-Madrid race of 1903. Shortly afterwards, racing authorities decided to use closed circuits.

The Brooklands Motor Course, the first of two specially-built tracks, opened in 1907. It had straight sections, hard corners, and steeply banked curves over which the cars raced at an alarming angle.

A little later a motor speedway was built in Indianapolis, USA. This track also had banked corners but was a much simpler course, consisting of an oval basin with all its corners laid out in the same direction. This is an artist's view of the American circuit.

MASERATI 250F

Opposite: Today, the rules of Formula 1, or Grand Prix Racing, allow the use of an engine of up to three litres. This regulation has changed over the years as power units have become more efficient. If the rules had not been constantly changed, motor racing may have become too dan-

gerous, defeating one of its main objects, that of helping to improve the design and safety of the more ordinary cars that we drive on the public highway.

In 1954, when the engine capacity size limit was set at 2.5 litres, the Italian company of Maserati asked engineer Gioacchino Colombo, who had already designed cars for Alfa Romeo and racing stable Ferrari, to build what was to become one of the most famous of Grand Prix racing cars, the Maserati 250F.

It was an elegant car, some say the most beautiful vehicle ever made for motor racing. Although it was not tremendously powerful or unusual in any other way, it seemed to have a special quality of grace and speed. It lapped Silverstone circuit in the hands of a private owner only two seconds slower than world champion Fangio in his Mercedes-Benz, and was seen out in front in many races during its early racing years.

In 1956 Stirling Moss drove his Maserati 250F to six Grand Prix victories and Fangio drove a 250F to his 1957 World Championship.

The car was powered by a six cylinder in-line engine of conventional operation. Taking advantage of the new Formula 1 that was coming into use, the car was ran on an alcohol-based fuel that gave it a power output of 244 bhp.

WOLF

Above: By the Seventies, Grand Prix racing was mainly the
province of small, specialist companies, few of which were
involved in the manufacture of road-going cars, as previous
generations of motor car manufacturers had been.

A new team which entered the lists in 1976 was that of
Wolf, which took its name from Walter Wolf, an Austro-
Canadian oil-rig millionaire. He began it by buying up the
Hesketh team, founded by Britain's Lord Hesketh, who had
spent much of his personal fortune on the quest for Grand
Prix racing success.

Like most contenders, the Wolf team used the Ford-
Cosworth V8 engine, but Wolf spent lavishly on talent,
engineers, and on drivers such as Jody Scheckter, who is
seen at the wheel in the picture. Scheckter, a South African,
began by driving karts at the age of 11 and progressed via
motor cycles to cars. Arriving in 1971 in Europe, he was at
first fast but undisciplined, but settled down to become a
formidable driver who in 1979 achieved the ultimate
accolade as World Champion.

For Wolf the 1979 season of Formula 1 racing was not
an entire success—some people said 'In like a Wolf, out
like a lamb'—and his drivers bid for the World Championship title faded away in mid season.

BLUE FLAME

Below: Gary Gabelich, a former test astronaut, became the fastest man on land in 1970 piloting a rocket-powered car across the salt flats at Bonneville, Utah, at 1014.5 km/h (630.38 mph). The car, called Blue Flame because it was sponsored by the American natural gas industry, had a rocket motor similar to those used in the space programme, burning liquified natural gas and hydrogen peroxide. The car was 9 m (30 ft) long and Gabelich rode in a cockpit in front of a 2.5 m (8ft) tall tail fin.

The land speed record, previously held by jet engined cars, fell to the rocket car after five weeks of frustration during which time the glowing tail set fire to the cords of the parachute that provided the car's braking power.

LOTUS

Left: The Formula One racing car in which Great Britain's Graham Hill became World Champion Driver in 1968 was strikingly different in appearance from all of its predecessors in Grand Prix racing.

The first difference was in the livery of the car. Lotus had pioneered the blazoning of advertising on racing cars in Europe, but in 1968 they went further and the cars were painted in red and gold to match the sponsoring company's cigarette packets. Since then advertising slogans have become a regular feature on the racing scene.

The second difference was in the aerofoil, or wing, fitted at the back of the car to help keep it on the ground at great speeds. It was so successful that the following year all F1 cars grew wings, though they were banned for a short while after two Lotus' shed theirs in the Spanish Grand Prix. However, the authorities later relented and, subject to regulations governing size, they have been used in motor races ever since.

The Lotus 49B of 1968 had a Ford-Cosworth DFV engine, a light alloy V8 unit of 2993 cc giving 430 hp at 10,000 rpm, which was to dominate racing for years. The body was an aluminium alloy monocoque with a glass fibre-detachable nose.

LOTUS

Far left: Another innovation in road-holding came to Grand Prix racing in 1978; it was the skirt.

Aerofoils help keep a car on the ground by creating pressure from above; the skirt or flaps, reaching to the ground, help create a vacuum under the car and hold it down by suction. Colin Chapman's Lotus team pioneered the idea and found speed on bends could be greatly increased. Other manufacturers followed Lotus' example in using skirts, but the 1978 World Championship went to Italian-American Lotus driver, Mario Andretti, who scored six victories.

FERRARI

Lower left: Ferrari has been a Grand Prix contender continuously since 1948, longer than any other racing team. It was founded by Enzo Ferrari, who raced Alfa Romeo cars in the Twenties and, though it is now controlled by Fiat, it is as sturdily independent as ever.

In an age when most racing cars are assembled from kits, Ferrari is unusual in making all its major components including the engine which is a flat twelve cylinder. It is also unusual in retaining its blood-red paintwork, the traditional racing livery of Italy, despite lucrative induce-

ments from advertisers to change.

Argentinian driver Carlos Reutemann, pictured here at the wheel, won four of Ferrari's five Grand Prix victories in 1978.

BRABHAM

Above: Australian Jack Brabham made sure of his place in motor racing history in 1966 when he became the first driver to win the World Championship in a car of his own make.

He had won the World Championship in 1959 and 1960, when driving a Cooper-Climax, but in 1961 he decided to build and race his own cars. His championship in 1966 was followed by that of Denny Hulme, a New Zealander, also driving a Brabham.

His cars have never been as successful since, though he is another constructor who has chosen to avoid the Ford-Cosworth engine used by most of the competition, opting in recent years for an Alfa Romeo 12-cylinder engine.

Brabham retired from driving in 1970 when he was 44 and 'the grand old man' of sport. The 1977 car in the picture is driven by the Brazilian, Carlos Pace.

TYRRELL-FORD

Top: The quest for better road-holding in Grand Prix motor racing led in 1976 to the six-wheel car, introduced by Ken Tyrrell, who had established his own team in 1970 with its own Ford-engined cars. Four wheels at the front and two at the back increased the tyre contact area, thereby improving braking and steering, while smaller front wheels reduced the wind-buffeting frontal area.

South African Jody Scheckter and France's Patrick Depailler (pictured at the wheel) scored a one-two victory in Sweden in 1976 but overall the six-wheeler was not really a success.

IN YOUR GARAGE

Open the garage door of any house in any part of the world, from Maine to Manchester, and you'll find the pride and joy of the family—the motor car. Part of the daily scene, part of the family life, part of modern history and the most important purchase a person ever makes, next to his home, the automobile has been in our garages now, in its millions, for well over half a century.

In France the chances are you'll find a Renault or a Citroën, the largest selling cars of that country. In Germany you'd find a Volkswagen (more VWs have been bought than any other car in the world), a Mercedes or an Opel. In Britain the odds are you'd find a Ford Cortina, still the United Kingdom's top-selling car. In Italy the middle range of Fiats, products of the largest company *of any sort* in Italy, takes pride of place.

Twenty five years ago the insignia on the radiators behind the garage door would have been quite different. You'd have seen marques like Frazer-Nash, Jowett, Sunbeam-Talbot (the distinguished name of Talbot has recently returned to grace a line

MERCEDES 280S

Mercedes-Benz tend to have long production runs, and the security of knowing that his car will look like the latest model for some time is comforting to a new owner. When a change of style or model arrives, it is usually a large step forward in design, not just a few body-trim changes, that tell other people that your present car is a year or two out of date.

You may notice that this Mercedes 280S did not roll off the production line last week—but how old is it? It would surprise most people to learn that the 2.7-litre 280S saloon could have left the factory in Germany as early as 1977, so little changed is its appearance today.

of cars), Riley, Standard, Humber to name but a few of the traditional names from British manufacturers alone.

Earlier still an open garage door would have shown even more exotic names. In the United States for instance you'd have seen—blazoned on the grilles, Nash, Studebaker, Moon, Star, Auburn, Case or Chandler, and of course the everlasting names of Ford, Chevrolet and Cadillac.

What was happening in France half a century ago? The automotive products of the leading motoring nation were also more varied then and included Mathis, Panhard (the oldest of them all), Citroën (just ten years old in 1929), Peugeot, Unic (Europe's taxi), Berliet, Leon Bolle, Aries, and of course Renault, even then France's mainstream producer.

In Italy it was always Fiat first, and in the Twenties, you'd find Alfa Romeo for the sporting family, Lancia, Ceirano, Ansaldo, Bianchi, and in a few of the grander garages, perhaps an Isotta-Fraschini or two. In Germany 50 years ago, the Volkswagen had not yet stolen the scene; Opel was Germany's best-seller and many household garages would be sheltering the little green Laubfrosch, Opel's popular Tree-Frog car.

The latest figures show that for good or ill, the world's motor makers are still pouring a continuous stream of cars into our garages—and it seems we are still able to afford to buy them. Germany's latest annual production figure is a staggering 3,890,000. France follows with 3,111,000 and Italy and Britain make about half that number. But the USA and Japan are the largest producers of all, the latter making some six million automobiles every year.

FORD ZEPHYR MK III

Top: The comparison with 'a gentle breeze' (the dictionary definition of a zephyr) might have been a little far-fetched, but the Zephyr was in its time a much-admired car; and there are still some, lovingly tended, on the roads of Britain today.

Its era was 1962-6, though as its mark number suggests, it had predecessors.

Ford opened in Britain in 1911, during the heyday of the Model T—but until 1932 the cars made in England were simply right-hand drive versions of American Fords. That changed when new works were opened at Dagenham, Essex which is still the company's headquarters in England. Then they began to make the first true British Fords. The company introduced the Zephyr, then the Ford 'Flagship' in '1951. It had a six-cylinder engine of 2262 cc in a slab-sided integral body frame. It was also equipped with 12-volt electrics.

Both Zephyr and the Zodiac had Ford Dearborn styled body work which was not always appreciated in the British market, but did not prevent the two models from selling in vast numbers. In 1963 the various Ford models of the time gave way in popularity to the new Cortina.

The Mark I Zephyr and its de luxe brother, the Zodiac, which followed, went on until 1956 when they were re-styled. Overdrive and automatic transmission were made available at this time.

Then in 1962 the Mark III arrived; the one pictured retained the six-cylinder engine, though a four-cylinder version was also available. It was replaced in 1966 by the Mark IV which had a new V-engine of $2\frac{1}{2}$ litres and a new design, with a bigger, flatter bonnet-top, much more modern in appearance. Yet the Mark III is still remembered with affection by those who owned, or just hoped to own, one.

VOLKSWAGON GOLF & POLO

Right and above: The famous Volkswagen 'Beetle' with its air-cooled, rear-mounted engine was for years the world's biggest selling car, but by the start of the Seventies it was out-dated and VW quickly had to produce a replacement. In 1974 the company began the introduction of a new range which could hardly have been more different from the old Beetle. The new VWs were water-cooled, front-engined, front-wheel-drive hatch-backs.

They were headed by the Golf—small-bodied, yet able to carry five people and with fold-down rear seating which enabled it to be turned into a semi-estate car with a surprisingly large load space. The standard engine is a four-cylinder 1093 cc though there are also engines of 1457 cc and 1588 cc.

The cars are seen in production in Germany in the picture above left. In 1976 the Golf was followed by the Polo (seen here in the snow) identical in its styling but even smaller, with a standard engine of only 895 cc, giving 132 km/h (82 mph) and a fuel-saving 38.7 mpg. It may also be fitted with 1093 cc and 1272 cc engines.

In 1978 came the Derby, a Polo with a boot, completing a winning range of small cars.

Today the top of the Polo range is the Polo GLS. This has a little more power than the standard models and has a top speed of 140 km/h (88 mph).

AUDI 80

Above: A motoring writer once observed that the Audi 80 was: 'Nothing but a Volkswagen Passat with snob appeal.' The explanation is that while Audi is considered to make some of Europe's better cars, distinguished in appearance and well-engineered, and therefore selling to the 'up-market' buyer, the firm was taken over by Volkswagen as long ago as 1964. However, the two cars look very dissimilar from one another.

The smart Audi 80 is a five-seater saloon with front-wheel drive. A four-cylinder 1272 cc engine gives it 145 km/h (90 mph) performance, but it can also be equipped with a 1588 cc engine which will take it to a swift 181 km/h (112 mph).

One of its unusual features is a steering stabilizing system which will maintain a straight-ahead line even with a tyre blow-out or uneven braking pressures. This feature can be a life-saver if a blow-out occurs on a motorway.

The Audi, a slightly upmarket car, holds fourth position in market popularity in Germany, its home country, with 1978 sales of 171,484. This figure was exceeded only by Ford, Opel and, holding firmly to the top place, Volkswagen.

PRINCESS

Above: In the Fifties the Austin Princess was a large and stately limousine, much used as a chauffeur-driven hire car for weddings, funerals and board meetings when a Rolls-Royce or Daimler would have been too expensive. How the Princess has changed!

Since 1975 the name has been applied to a wedge-shaped saloon, one of the British Leyland range, though it has some pretensions to being a cut above the mere bread-and-butter models.

Interconnected Hydragas suspension units give a smooth and comfortable ride for four or five passengers, and the driver's seat can be adjusted for height and tilt as well as normal reach and rake.

The car has front-wheel drive and the engine is transverse-mounted. The basic power unit is a modest four-cylinder 1695 cc which will propel the car at 159 km/h (99 mph) but there are also more energetic versions with a four-cylinder 1993 cc unit and a six-cylinder 2227 cc unit. The latter gives a top speed of 170 km/h (106 mph).

AUSTIN ALLEGRO 1500 SPECIAL

Above Right: A typical Leyland bread-and-butter car of the Seventies, the Allegro was introduced in 1973. It is conventional, undistinguished, yet efficient, reasonably comfortable and economical on fuel—just what is wanted by so many family motorists.

The Allegro is a four-to-five seater with two or four doors. Like the Princess, it has a transverse engine driving the front wheels, and Hydragas suspension—gas-filled and sealed for life.

The 1500 model is one of nine ranging from an 1100 to a 1750 cc. Its engine is a four-cylinder of 1485 cc giving the car a maximum speed of 148 km/h (92 mph). Unusually, it is fitted with a five-speed gearbox.

The Special—a *de luxe* version of the standard saloon—provides a vinyl roof, twin reversing lights, a central console with a clock, and a locking glove-box.

VAUXHALL CHEVETTE GL

Top: Britain's Vauxhall company is a part of America's General Motors corporation, and the Chevette was launched in 1975 as the first of a series of 'worldwide' GM models designed to have many body components in common. For example, the suspension and steering came from the Opel Kadett. Opel is another division of General Motors and has its headquarters near Frankfurt in Germany.

The GL is one of ten Chevette models, a three-door hatch-back of the kind which achieved great popularity in the mid-Seventies, with a counter-balanced tailgate opening onto a surprisingly large load space, with the rear seat folded.

The engine, an improved version of that used in the Vauxhall Viva, is a four-cylinder of 1256 cc with the drive to the rear wheels. The top speed is 146 km/h (91 mph). Distinctive features of the Chevette are the rectangular, recessed headlamps.

FORD FIESTA

Left: The car being so carefully washed by these children is the British Ford company's first baby car, its answer to the ageing British Leyland Mini which was launched in 1959. Although the Ficsta is aimed at the first-time car buyer, it is slightly more luxurious than the Mini.

It was long-awaited. Ford made no secret of the fact that, as a latecomer to the hatch-back scene, it had been examining all its rivals' products. The lessons learned enabled Ford to provide, amongst other improvements, a better driving position and better visibility than the Mini. It was finally launched in 1977. It measures just 356 cm in length (just over $11\frac{1}{2}$ ft).

A three-door car, it came, as usual with Fords, in a range of ten different choices of specifications. The Fiesta S seen here has a 1117 cc transverse-mounted engine driving the front wheels, and a top speed of 145 km/h (90 mph) or a 1298 cc engine giving a top speed of 158 km/h (98 mph). Features of the S include stiffened suspension, a rev counter and a clock.

By 1980 the Fiesta had become a highly successful Ford product, climbing towards its second million sales. It was quickly offered in a number of guises—the Fiesta L with the 957cc engine, the Fiesta 1.1 L with an 11.17cc engine and various additions, the sportive 1.1 S and the 1.3 S which is their top sportive model.

The Fiesta has been entered in motor sports of various types, and has proved to be reasonably successful. But its greatest asset with today's ever-increasing labour costs is its low servicing cost and the fact that it is a fairly simple piece of engineering for which the service time is drastically reduced.

The car's handling is good. It is light and steers well, whilst the ride is good on all but the most poor surface. It has an economical mileage—about 32 mpg in a commuting situation and up to 41 mpg at a restrained cruising speed.

SHANGAI

Above: This is a rare glimpse of the current model of the Shanghai, a fairly large family saloon, in its homeland, the People's Republic of China. First seen in 1958, when it was called the Phoenix, the Shanghai has a conventional six-cylinder engine of 2.3-litres. The gearbox is still only three-speed, somewhat old-hat today, and its front-end appearance is some ten years behind the design trends of Western manufacturers' modern products.

The Shanghai factory is small by our standards, with 2,000 workers making 4,000 cars and about 3,000 small trucks a year. Private cars are still an unusual sight in China, and most of the vast town populations travel by bicycle. The model seen here was launched in 1971.

SAAB TURBO

Top Right: The motoring press regarded the Swedish turbo-charged Saab as the best car in production when it was first seen in 1977. The power comes from a two-litre four-cylinder engine boosted by a turbo-charger that runs only when it is needed— for acceleration and uphill gradients. A tiny turbine is driven by the exhaust gases from the engine. An air compressor mounted on the same shaft turns with it. The compressor delivers an air/fuel mixture into the cylinder at higher pressure than would normally be drawn in by the pixton's suction. The extra air and fuel supply thus produce more energy on every piston power-stroke.

RED FLAG

Right: In the Republic of China this car is called a Hongki, which sounds a little odd in English but means 'Red Flag' in its native land. The Hongki is made in China's largest motor factory, at Changchung.

It is produced as a five-seater saloon or a seven-place limousine for official and ceremonial use. The car has a 5.6-litre V8 power unit with a claimed top speed of 192 km/h (120 mph).

SHANGAI

Far right: This older Shanghai, parked in a cool and tree-lined avenue in Canton, is about the size of the now discontinued Triumph 2000, with body lines that remind us of the 1950s.

China also makes the $2\frac{1}{2}$-litre Peking BJ 750, the most modern of that country's vehicles. Its pleasant, clean lines are quite similar to several Western cars including the 1980 Cortina.

15-05760

AMERICAN AUTOS

The twin problems of pollution and fuel scarcity have exercised the knowledge and the conscience of engineers in the United States for many years.

Pollution was the first enemy, attacking parts of the USA in the form of smog, these foggy fumes, unwanted products of the internal combustion engine that hang over a busy city. Soon researchers were at work designing engines that emitted fewer unburnt and toxic gases.

The apparently sudden diminution of the world's energy was the next dramatic problem. The long distances and cheap gasoline of America had engendered larger and heavier cars during the years and compared with Europe's average engine size of some 1.5-litres, US engines had grown to around seven-litres.

These US gas-guzzlers had to go, and with typically American energy, engineers who for years had been designing bigger and bigger heavyweights, quickly began lopping off bits of their new designs, 'down-sizing' their cars. Now most US cars are shorter, lighter and less fuel-thirsty. America's new environmental rules say that all cars should give an average of nineteen miles to the US gallon, and the industry is now geared to produce cars that conform to this regulation.

American Motors, the smallest of the main manufacturers are already a jump ahead. For some years they have been making smaller cars than most with a view to future trends, and the gamble has paid off. On pages 68 and 69 some of their small but very advanced models are shown. It is a fair guess that this will be the design trend of future US automobiles.

CHRYSLER NEW YORKER FIFTH AVE

The flagship of the Chrysler range must surely take the prize for the longest name ever given to an automobile. Although this new model is the most expensive of Chrysler products, it is offered to the public only in the colours seen here. Just as Henry Ford said way back in the 1920s when orders for his Model T were pouring in: 'They can have it in any colour they like—so long as it's black!' There's one comfort for purchasers, though. The white-walled tyres have a gold lining! To cut fuel consumption all US manufacturers reduced the size of their new cars during 1979, including this model which has had 25 cm lopped off its length.

LINCOLN

Four Passenger Coupe

AUBURN

Top: On the front of the grille are the figures '852' showing that this was one of the last models of this famous American trend-setter of the 1930s. The Auburn, first made in 1900, had always been a hand-built car with a flair for fashion and speed, but its maker's fortunes had always been rather fragile. The 851 and 852 were schoolboys' dreams, with long tapering bonnets, raked windscreens and tiny two-some cockpits, slick, curved wings and body-covering. The super-charger and huge flexible exhaust pipes completed the picture of the young sportsman's car. Each of these cars carried a small plaque confirming that the car had been tested before sale.

LINCOLN FOUR PASSENGER COUPE

Left: This Lincoln coupé of grandfather's day is as exotic as the bird hovering over it in the poster—or so the makers would have us believe. Since 1922 the American Lincoln had been part of the US Ford company, a sort of superior Model T at first, which later had a prestige of its own. It was always a separate car-making concern using only Ford money and expertise. Named after Abraham Lincoln, the car became known as the 'President's car' after President Coolidge bought one in 1924, forging a bond with the White House which is still firm today. The car was made in a bewildering number of styles in the '20s—a club roadster, sport roadster, touring, coupé, sedan (saloon) and a large limousine for the wealthy motorist.

FORD MUSTANG

Above left: The story of the US Ford Mustang began with its ancestor the Thunderbird, the sporting Ford of the 1950s, competing with Chevrolet's rakish Corvette. Time for a change came in 1964 when Ford captured the imagination of the youth of America with the Mustang. This was a sporty-looking car with close-coupled four seats, using a 4.7-litre V8 engine or a 3.3-litre six cylinder—and enough power to please genuine sports fans. Ford sold half a million in the first six months, all over the world. This 1979 model, has a more subdued appearance in line with present motoring safety and economy trends.

AMC SPIRIT LIFTBACK

Top: By 1979 America was deep in the energy crisis and car manufacturers were faced with demands to produce fuel economy models. The large 'gas guzzler' automobiles were on the point of being outlawed.

American Motor Corporation Spirit Liftback was a redesigned version of an earlier, small ('sub-compact') car, the Gremlin—a curious name since gremlins are allegedly mischievous imps responsible for all sorts of mechanical faults.

American Motors claimed the new car was a luxury compact rather than an economy model and said it was geared to the youth market. It was certainly trendy, and also modest in size by American standards at 428 cm (14 ft), a two-door four-seater with a top speed of 136 km/h (85 mph) and a fuel consumption of 26.4 mpg. There were, however, faster six- and eight-cylinder models ranging up to 4982 cc capacity and 165 km/h (103 mph) performance.

CONCORD STATION WAGON

Above right: The Concord was also modest for an American station wagon at 472 cm (15½ ft) in length for a five- seater, and had a fuel consumption of 21.6 mpg, a very economical figure from a six-cylinder 3802 cc engine.

The car kept the traditional wood panel effect associated with station wagons (the US term for estate car).

Traditional features of American cars such as automatic transmission, power steering, tinted glass, air conditioning and a sunshine roof were all optional extras. Austerity was becoming standard in 1979.

The Concord is also available with four-cylinder and eight-cylinder engines and in sedan and hatch-back versions.

AMC PACER LIMITED

Right: A third American Motors series in 1979 was the Pacer. A two-door hatch-back it looks strangely, but not unattractively, both squat and high for its length of 439 cm (under 14½ ft), mainly due to its low waistline.

This four-seater, with a 154 km/h (96 mph) top speed is slightly more thirsty than other AMC cars. A consumption of 20.5 mpg is within existing US Congress requirements though it misses the target of 27.5 mpg set for 1985. Big changes are taking place in American gasoline consumption due to the world oil shortage, that is even forcing the Americans to reduce the amount of fuel they use.

The Pacer offers the same optional features as the Concord, plus a rear window washer/wiper (highly desirable on a hatch-back, as the partial vacuum its shape creates at the rear attracts spray) as extras. It is also produced in an eight-cylinder 4982 cc version.

American - United
AMC

CADILLAC LE MANS

Left above: The Cadillac company, founded by Henry Leland with a high quality single-cylinder car, was taken over in 1909 by General Motors, becoming the world's biggest producer of automobiles. Cadillac's role was—and is—to supply the top end of the market, the 'carriage trade', whilst following contemporary fashions.

In the Fifties the trend was to chrome, particularly at the front end, as the picture shows. Many American, and later European models featured these 'rhino tusks' or dramatic 'Japanese Grin' grilles. This model was no sports car, as understood in Europe, but a typically massive American tourer with a V8 engine of 5424 cc and a windscreen which foreshadowed the panoramic wrap-around screens to come.

BUICK SUPER

Left below: William Durant, the founder of General Motors, incorporated Buick, started by Scottish immigrant David Dunbar Buick, into his empire in 1908. It served a more popular market than Cadillac and its styling excesses in the Fifties were even more grotesque.

The chrome bars on this Buick were supposed to combine the functions of radiator grille and bumper (fender). In theory it was no more costly to replace individual damaged bars than to replace a fender but this proved incorrect. The toothy fashion lasted for several years.

The cars had 4.1- or 5.2-litre straight-eight engines, replaced in 1953 by V8s.

DODGE MAGNUM

Top: Though a 1979 car, the Dodge Magnum seems to belong to an older generation of mass-produced American cars—a two-door, six-seater, 548 cm (18 ft) long with automatic transmission and a top speed of 165 km/h (103 mph). It has a consumption of 19.2 mpg, and a thirstier 5900 cc version is capable of up to 190 km/h (118 mph). Like the AMC models it offers a glittering range of optional extras.

DODGE OMNI

Above left: The Dodge Omni, a name said to have been inspired by the film, Star Wars, is practically European in its moderate thirst. It has a tiny (by US standards) four-cylinder engine of 1714 cc giving a top speed of 146 km/h (91 mph) for a return of 30.1 mpg.

It is also a tiny car by American standards. The four door four-seat hatch-back pictured, with its slope-nosed front and fast-back rear, is only 419 cm (little more than 13½ ft) long, though, curiously, the two-door version is slightly longer.

This could indeed be the shape of American cars to come.

PONTIAC FIREBIRD TRANS-AM

Top: America still builds a few traditional models like this two-door four-seater hard top coupé with its big, lazy, eight-cylinder 6604 cc engine and automatic transmission. It has 180 km/h (112 mph) performance but gives only 16.8 mpg.

There is also a faster eight-cylinder model in the range, and there are also smaller-engined versions.

At Detroit, America's great motor manufacturing centre in Michigan, they say that all the new 'down-sized' cars that are being made today and those that are on the drawing board for the late 1980s have as much room inside as the old six-seater 'big sleds' with their enormous V engines. This Trans-Am is the 1980 model, basically the same design as its predecessor but with redesigned front and rear ends, making it look even hotter than the old Firebird.

CADILLAC BROUGHAM D'ELEGANCE

Above right: Cadillac has for years been the American Rolls-Royce and an international symbol of wealth. One hardly expects a sub-compact from Cadillac and this Fleetwood is certainly not a small car.

It is 562 cm (nearly $18\frac{1}{2}$ ft) long has a mighty eight-cylinder 6964 cc engine and automatic transmission. It has a speed of 181 km/h (115 mph) and likes to drink a gallon of gas every 26.8 kilometres (16.8 miles). This is the sort of car Americans are becoming concerned about in a period of diminishing fuel supplies.

For an unashamedly luxury car it has the unusual feature of a bench front seat (possibly to allow for a security guard).

It also has electrically-operated windows and air conditioning. It can be bought with fuel injection, and there are other models in the range including a coupé, a sedan and what Cadillac calls 'a formal limousine'. This car may possibly be the last of the line of US 5000-pounder heavyweights.

INDEX

ACKNOWLEDGMENTS

The author and publishers would like to thank the following persons and organisations for their help in producing this book: Ford Motor Co. Ltd; Mrs Sheila Knapman; Mercedes-Benz (UK) and Mrs Salmon; Daimler-Benz AG; General Motors; Rolls-Royce Motors; British Leyland; Adam Opel; Lips Autotron, Holland; Citroën; Aston Martin Lagonda; Lotus Group; Fiat and Lancia; Mr Graham Marks; Datsun UK; BMW; Mr Paul Roberts of Cardiff; Mr Nick Wright; Mr Cecil Bendall; Regie Renault; Volkswagen; American Motors; Mr Stephen Manley, Newport; Goodyear Tyre and Rubber Co; London Art Tech.; Maranello Concessionaires Ltd; Chrysler Corporation, Detroit; Mrs Gina Corrigan, Occidor; Saab.